WHISPERS OF THE HEART: A COLLECTION OF LOVE POEMS

EXPRESSING THE DEPTHS OF EMOTION

SATYAM RANJAN

I would like to express my sincerest gratitude to all the readers of "Whispers of the Heart: A Collection of Love Poems." Your support and encouragement mean the world to me. This book is a reflection of my personal experiences, and I hope that it resonates with you in some way. Thank you for taking the time to read my words and for allowing me to share my heart with you. I hope that my poetry brings you joy, comfort, and a deeper understanding of the human experience of love.

Contents

Foreword   *vii*

Preface   *ix*

Acknowledgements   *xi*

Prologue   *xiii*

1. The Mystery Of Love   1

2. The Lessons Of One Sided Love   3

3. The Weight Of Unrequited Love   4

4. The Worth Of A Wonder   5

5. Unspoken Affection   7

6. A Game Of Love   9

7. Path To The Horizon   11

8. A Day Of Sorrows   13

9. Love's Journey And Enduring   14

10. A Second Chance   15

A Final Note On Love   17

Foreword

As a reader, I was immediately drawn in by the raw emotion and vulnerability present in "Whispers of the Heart: A Collection of Love Poems." Satyam Ranjan has a unique ability to capture the complexities of love and relationships in verse, and their words resonate with readers on a deep level. Each poem is a reflection of the author's personal experiences, making this collection relatable and relatable.

The imagery in these poems is vivid and evocative, painting a picture of love in all its forms. From the first flutter of attraction to the deep, abiding love of a lifetime, Satyam Ranjan takes us on a journey through the depths of love and emotion.

This poetry collection is not just for the romantics, but for anyone who has ever felt the pull of the heartstrings. I highly recommend this book to anyone looking to understand the complexities of love and the human experience.

It's an honor for me to write a forward for this book and I can assure you that it's a must-read for anyone seeking to understand the power of love.

Preface

Love is a universal feeling that has inspired poets for centuries. This collection of love poems is a tribute to the beauty and complexity of this emotion. These poems explore the different facets of love, from the initial spark of attraction to the deep and lasting bond that can develop between two people. Some of the poems in this collection are joyful and celebratory, while others delve into the darker aspects of love and relationships. But all of them are honest and true, reflecting the many different ways that love can be experienced. Whether you're reading these poems to remember a past love or to find inspiration for your own writing, I hope that you'll find something in these pages that resonates with you. Enjoy the journey.

Acknowledgements

Writing this collection of love poems has been a journey of self-discovery and I would like to take a moment to acknowledge the people who have helped me along the way.

First and foremost, I would like to thank my family for their unwavering support and encouragement. They have always believed in me, even when I doubted myself. Their love and guidance has been invaluable.

I would also like to thank my friends who have been my sounding board and have shared in this journey with me. They have read, re-read, and provided feedback on my poems, which has helped me to refine my craft.

I would also like to thank my mentor and poetry teacher who has guided me through the process of turning my thoughts and feelings into verse. His wisdom and guidance has been invaluable.

Finally, I would like to thank all the readers who will take the time to read my collection of love poems. Your support and feedback means more than you can imagine.

Thank you all for being a part of my journey.

Prologue

Love is a mystery that has puzzled poets, philosophers, and scholars for centuries. It is a feeling that can inspire us to greatness, or bring us to our knees. It is a force that can change our lives forever. This collection of love poems is a journey through the many facets of this emotion.

These poems are a reminder that love can take many forms and is often found in unexpected places.

Whether you are reading to remember a past love, or to find inspiration for your own writing, I hope that these poems will lead you toward a deeper understanding of this mysterious and powerful emotion.

So, let us begin this journey together, and discover the many ways that love can touch our lives.

1. The Mystery of Love

Love is a rose that blooms in spring,
A gentle breeze that whispers sweet,
It's a dance that spins in circles,
And a song that skips a beat.
It's a light that shines in darkness,
A beacon in the night,
It's the warmth that fills the coldest days,
And makes everything feel right.
Love is the laughter that we share,
The tears we shed together,
It's the memories we make,
That last forever and ever.
It's the hand that holds us steady,
The arms that keep us strong,
It's the beating of two hearts,
That makes a beautiful song.
Love is a journey, a path unknown,
A mystery we'll unravel,
With every step we take together,
Our love will only travel.
It's a promise, a commitment,
A forever kind of thing,
Love is the one thing we can count on,
It's the truest of all things.

Satyam Ranjan

2. The Lessons of One Sided Love

One sided love, a bittersweet pain
Teaches me to love, but also to refrain
From putting all my heart, on just one shelf
For fear of loving someone, who cannot love myself
I thought I knew, what love was all about
But one sided love, made me want to shout
That love is not just feelings, deep and true
But also actions, that someone else must do
I used to think, that love was just a game
But now I know, it's not just fame
It's about give and take, and a mutual need
But one sided love, left me with just greed
But through this pain, I've learned and grown
I've become stronger, and more self-known
One sided love, may have left me scarred
But it's taught me to love, with a heart that's not barred
So though I may not have, the love I desire
I am changed, by the one sided love fire
And though it may have burned, it's made me new
A better person, in all that I do.
Satyam Ranjan

3. The Weight of Unrequited Love

A poor boy, with love in his heart
But unable to share, for fear of being torn apart
By the financial differences, that lay between
Him and the rich girl, his heart's queen
He watches from afar, as she goes about her days
Luxuries and riches, at her fingertips and gaze
He longs to tell her, of the love he holds dear
But the fear of rejection, keeps him in fear
For how can he compete, with all that she has
A poor boy, with nothing to offer, no land or cash
He knows that he could make her happy, with just his love
But societal norms, and financial means, rise above
And so he remains silent, and hides his love deep
Hoping that someday, she will learn to see
The person he is, and not the life he leads
And give him a chance, to fulfill his love's needs
But until then, he holds onto hope
That his love will be enough, to help him cope
With the pain of unrequited love, and the life he's made
A poor boy, in love with a rich girl, but forever weighed.
Satyam Ranjan

4. The Worth of a Wonder

An awesome girl with a heart of gold,
Loving and caring, never cold.
Intelligent and beautiful, too,
She's a woman who knows just what to do.
She's wise beyond her years,
And makes practical decisions based on her needs.
But she doesn't give away more than she should,
For she knows the value of being good.
She loves to travel to the hilltops high,
Where the air is crisp and the sky is night.
She takes in all the beauty around,
And revels in the peace she's found.
But despite all the amazing things she's done,
She doesn't understand her worth, not yet, not one.
She doesn't see just how incredible she is,
And the impact she has on those she's met.
But that's where this poem comes in,
To show her just how much she means to her kin.
For she's a one of a kind,
A beautiful, loving, intelligent mind.
And as the words wash over her,
Her eyes will fill with tears,
For she'll finally understand,
Just how much she's loved, and how grand.

So here's to you, amazing girl,
May these words help you twirl,
Into the realization,
Of just how truly incredible you are, and your realization.
Satyam Ranjan

5. Unspoken Affection

A girl of many charms
So calm, yet full of cheer
She brings laughter to the hearts
Of all who gather near
Naughty, yet with a heart so pure
She puts others before herself
Her careless ways so enduring
It's no wonder she's loved by all
She's a wanderer at heart
Her love for hills and valleys deep
But perhaps she's afraid to fall
For someone she may want to keep
Her interest in fashion clear
She's a girl of many talents
She's approachable and kind
It's no surprise she's so well liked
Though I'm just a friend, it's plain to see
She's a girl who's meant for greatness
Her beauty and her spirit shine
Like the stars that light the night's vastness
I'm grateful for her presence in my life
For the moments we have shared
But if my feelings were to be revealed
I fear it would be too much for her to bear

So I'll keep these feelings to myself
And silently admire from afar
Hoping that one day she'll understand
How much she means to me, how great her worth.
Satyam Ranjan

6. A Game of Love

With every game we play,
I may come out on top,
But in her eyes, I see a light,
That makes my heart stop.
For though she may not show it,
I know she loves to play,
And every time I ask her,
Her eyes light up in a special way.
But beneath her child-like laughter,
And her funny, playful ways,
Lies a heart that's been through pain,
And a soul that's seen dark days.
She's been forced to live with fear,
And bear the weight of pain,
But still she wears a smile,
And holds back her tears again.
But I want to be the one,
To take her hand in mine,
And help her leave the past behind,
And find the love she's been denied.
For she deserves to be happy,
And to know that she's not alone,
I'll be here for her always,
And help her find a home.

With every game we play,
I'll be her partner and her guide,
And help her heal and grow,
And be her rock by her side.
Satyam Ranjan

7. Path to the Horizon

In a world full of noise and distraction,

I find myself feeling lost and alone.

Depression weighs heavy on my mind,

Leaving me feeling empty and unknown.

Financially broke, with nothing to show,

Mentally drained, with no energy to grow.

Emotionally damaged, with a heart full of pain,

I try to find love, but it seems in vain.

A girl I adore, with all my heart,

But she does not see me, and we are worlds apart.

I try to move on, but the memories linger,

Leaving me stuck, in an eternal slumber.

I know not where my path will lead,

But I hope to find the strength to succeed.

Though the journey may be hard and long,

I'll keep moving forward, with a heart full of song.

Though shadows loom and doubts assail,

And heartache's sting and sorrow's wail,

Still to the horizon's distant gleam,

I'll lift my eyes and dare to dream.

For in the darkest of the night,

A glimmer shines, a guiding light.

And though the path may be obscured,

I'll find my way, my steps secured.

So let this poem be a spark,
To light the fire within your heart,
For though the road ahead may be long,
With strength and hope, you'll find your song.
Satyam Ranjan

8. A Day of Sorrows

The day was dark, my mood was low,
My relative's words cut like a knife,
I tried to help in every way,
But all my efforts brought her strife.
The extra bucks paid to the driver,
Were a small price for her comfort and ease,
But her words, they left me feeling drained,
My good intentions brought me to my knees.
As I walked, my heart was heavy,
A terrible accident I did behold,
My soul was shaken, my spirit weary,
As I struggled to handle all that was told.
And when I thought the day couldn't worsen,
My crush spoke words that cut like a blade,
She said that she did not feel the same,
And my heart, it shattered in the shade.
But through the pain and through the sorrow,
I'll keep my head held high with pride,
For I know that I acted with kindness,
And love is always worth the ride.
Satyam Ranjan

9. Love's Journey And Enduring

When first I saw her, my heart skipped a beat,
In that moment, my fate was sealed, complete.
As I approached her, my nerves began to shake,
But my determination to talk to her did not break.
When I asked her for her number, my palms were slick with sweat,
But her smile and nod, made my heart forget.
As we talked on the phone, my feelings grew,
With each word spoken, my love for her, anew.
As we talked regularly, my love for her did bloom,
And in my heart, her love for me, consumed.
But love is not always easy, and it's not always strong,
There are times when it's weak, and it feels so wrong.
But true love will endure, through the highs and the lows,
For when it's real, it will never let go.
So let us hold tight to our love, and never let it die,
For in the end, our love will reach the sky.
Satyam Ranjan

10. A second chance

With trembling hands, I wrote a note,
To say how sorry I was,
For all the hurt and pain I'd caused,
And hoped for her forgiveness.
But as I read it over,
I feared she'd never see
The depth of my remorse,
Or understand my plea.
But then she smiled and took my hand,
And said she'd let it go,
That she saw in me a future,
And a love that's yet to grow.
And in that moment, I knew,
That my obsession would turn to love,
For she was perfect in my eyes,
And I wanted her forevermore.
So let the past be in the past,
And let us start anew,
With open hearts and open minds,
And a love that's pure and true.
Satyam Ranjan

A Final Note On Love

Thank you for reading 'Whispers of the Heart: A Collection of Love Poems.' We hope that these words have touched your heart and sparked feelings of love and connection. We believe that love is one of the most powerful and transformative forces in the world, and it is our hope that these poems have helped to remind you of that. We hope that you will continue to find inspiration in the words of these poems and that they will be a reminder of the beauty and power of love in your life. Thank you again for your support, and happy reading.